A Private Anthology

Poems from the Heart

By

Joe Steier

Dedication

A Private Reflection is dedicated to the friends who were always there as foundational rocks along a complicated journey, spiritual advisors who shared their faith to help me find mine, and my amazing family who has always provided unconditional love from day 1.

Acknowledgement

Mrs. Nancy Eckert, my famed grade schoolteacher, who helped me overcome dyslexia and speech issues to learn basic poetry that I still use often today.

About the Author

This quick poetry read by Joe Steier, author of *My God! Your God?* is a reminder of the power of utilizing simple poetry to capture emotions that you never dealt with or unfinished feelings that you want closure on. This intimate reflection shows how we can reframe our thoughts, examine our past, leverage our complicated upbringings and overcome our own suffering by just writing it down as maybe our best therapy option.

Joe Steier is a long-term business entrepreneur and Hall of Fame Business Leader who has brought spirituality into the workplace as one of his foundational pillars as a co-founder of Signature Healthcare. He has launched many other business organizations and non-profits with a passion for learning disabilities, mental health support services, and homeless issues. He utilized stream-of-conscious writing as a leadership tool for executive coaching and introduced poetry reading often as a great tool to connect leaders in intimate ways as a form of collaborative sharing.

Prior to his business career, Joe overcame major dyslexia struggles in early education to earn various degrees, several masters, professional licenses, and an Ivy League doctorate in Education. His learning difficulty caused many private adolescent mental struggles, but passionate teachers pushed him to forget verbal or written perfection and learn to master self-expression as the highest form of communication where we can explore our deepest thoughts, explore contemplative thinking, and share with others to get recentered so we call to realize that "human suffering is a universal condition" for all of us to unpack.

Today, he still publishes various blogs, writes articles, teaches leadership classes, and is a successful public speaker at joesteier.com

Table of Contents

Joe Steier

Poem Book

Titled "A Private Anthology."

In a complicated time in man's evolutionary journey, I rediscovered an old reflective passion that I used when life overwhelmed me, and I needed an outlet to capture my feelings. After the pandemic decimated many of us and changed our lives in ways we never saw coming, I wanted to find a way to unpack all that happened and learn to talk to myself again.

I returned to my late teen passion: stream-of-consciousness poetry writing using simple rhyme schemes as couplets in many cases and some alternating rhyming schemes as well.

For all of us today, I feel like anything we say can upset another party in this divided time, but poetry has the rarest ability to express our private feelings and where they came from to give all of us context to underreact to the headlines but share our journeys in a way that we can actually hear each other without the noise.

In this small release, I did not release all my poems in a short, quick-read book called "A Private Anthology," which is just a few of my favorites that I wrote post-pandemic. There were a few poems from special occasions that I published to share with large audiences to explain how I really felt at that moment in time, and I think they are still relevant, even today.

On a light note, I sprinkled in a few I wrote with my oldest daughter, Jacqueline, from over a decade ago when we used to write poems at night as wannabe artists that she drafted between ages ten and twelve. These might provide you with some insight into how we can use poetry with young children as a way to better express their changing feelings in a healthy way that will expand the conversation.

Remember, I suffer from dyslexia, so this is not Arnold's *Dover Beach*!

As a student, I loved reading Emily Dickinson's work because of their crisp, to-the-point, powerful works. It helped me control my young adolescent anxiety, which is when I first started writing poetry to package my emotions over a decade-long process. I memorized many of the works in order to never lose the cadence or the feelings she gave me as a young person who often was very lost. I can still recite Number 112 – "Success is Counted Sweetest" as a reminder of how winning and losing are still part of a bigger process, but they feel so different at the time.

I had these premature fears of death from my late childhood and really became attached to *Ithaca* by Cavafy, the famed Greek Poet, because I was so overly ambitious that that masterpiece would help me slow down and not lose sight of the unique journey we are all on. I found that during the passing of Jacqueline Kennedy, it was read at her funeral. That poem helped me not to embrace the goals that seemed so important at the time but to embrace the pain and joy of the journey. I kept that printout in my Bible or journal all the time to remind myself to find the knowledge, enjoy the people, and embrace the experiences (good or bad). This is just another example of how much poetry was used to control and expand my emotions privately.

As an adult, I use poetry in leadership classes as a sharing experience when we read classics aloud and discuss them as a group with confidentiality. In this adult process, I fell in love with Robert Penn Warren, who had small-time Kentucky roots that made us all feel a connection to his integration of the natural and the spiritual intersections. Honestly, I still use his poems in various workshops and highlight his masterpiece "Delusion? – No!" as the most used work for a great discussion. I placed it in the back of the appendix for you to try out.

After the passing of my mother, I lost my poetry journal from college and from my professional travels in my twenties, which had hundreds of simple works that helped me through challenging times. I still search for it often, with no success. I wanted to write lyrics for music but pivoted to stream-of-consciousness poetry writing at the time; rap was changing music with simple rhymes. Losing your two-decade private work is scary because I worry about who might find it now. Privately, it is like losing your diary because you can never know who might discover it.

Either way, I decided to write again as non-medication therapy after some recent setbacks and painful losses that I never really dealt with, and after helping Signature HC as a CEO through the COVID pandemic was a devasting experience for so many of our amazing residents, passionate caregivers, and our Signature communities.

Remember: this style of poetry is not about perfection or complicated literary structures. This is about getting your feelings out freely and in the simplest manner so that your emotions can compound and go deeper within yourself, transferring you to a peaceful state. These are not things we easily talk about at a dinner party but something we can share in a way with others to better understand who we are. My sincere hope is to get others to open back up and start unpacking all that has happened to us as a new way to perform "self-care" for our souls.

All of the book proceeds are going to the **Signature Foundation, a 501C3 that provides emergency funding for frontline caregivers at Signature Healthcare, funds "dream vacations" for the residents at Signature Healthcare communities and provides**

scholarships for high-achieving stakeholders at Signature Healthcare.

1. God. Family. Freedom. Country

I have not clearly seen it (on a big wall) like that in years!

But when I did it brought me to tears!

We stood there for a long moment, just trying to take it all in.

But my mind wondered to the rugged coast that could have been the bloody end.

It is hard to bridge all that transpired in that epic season.

But we know now for what reason.

If all that sacrificed could leave their marked graves for just one day.

What do we all think might be their final say?

Did they save the boldest innovative idea of all time?

Or defend a sacred text that is impossible to really define?

They might ask us all to come back together quickly, to ward off evil again.

So, we don't have to wonder what it might have been:

The Nobel order seems to shift over extended periods of debate.

But at least Founding Fathers knew to keep a half-wall between church & state.

They may have counted all who perished defending their own sacred scroll.

Knowing they had to protect the original soul.

A quick civic refresher course may be needed for all of us today.

Just a reminder that no one is allowed to just pick your favorite act of the masterpiece play.

If the first two are deeply personal to everyone who is part of the one-of-a-kind plan.

Many thought the third one would bring us together to take a collective last stand.

Remember, they all predicted there would be setbacks along these uncharted attacks, but never a reason to ever turn back!

Written on the way to OKC on May 1st, 2023

2. Heritage

Early defenders fought so hard, so it never just fades away,

yet not true for the ones who never had their own say.

Imagery and tapestry were soothing as we looked far and wide—

yet everyone knows now from what side.

We can rewrite all of the stories, so everyone has a new day,

all in a process to show there might be a better way.

King, Kennedy, Davis, Ali, Jefferson, just to name a few,

but most likely it might have been the whole crew.

Machiavellian's *The Prince* told us they all might become corrupt from within.

Where do you think he had actually been?

If imperfection or mistakes were made along every blazoned path,

when does everyone now say they need a clean bath?

Now when we all go back into that historical lens,

all you hear about now are colossal sins.

Celebrated, cancelled or just taken down,

they all just hope no one makes a sound.

Does everyone feel better, or just become more pissed off?

All of this, at what real cost?

Absolute truth will never be the main part,

until we all realize it was never a fresh start.

It may just all disappear slowly like a rough tide,

until the stories are controlled by the other side.

Many are so confused now that they've become scared to join in,
knowing they might be entering their own lion's den.
Is it ignorance, progress, or just paranormal bliss?
I can't remember when we all had that last kiss.

Written as a reflection after the removal of the King Louis XVI Statue in Louisville, Kentucky, after being vandalized during city protests in 2020

3. Absolute Truth

Plato and Aristotle both claimed that Absolute Truth should be the lifelong quest for us all.

Or do you think they both knew, for most of us, it could be our biggest fall?

Plato's foundational work was supposed to let us initially see beyond what was obvious to our eyes,

so did he hope that the ethereal imagery and thoughts were never really in disguise?

The Republic warned us that a private cave might change what we thought we knew—

so he could eliminate what we thought was previously true?

With all of us having to leave so much chained to the wall,

Aristotle knew someone would need to answer the call!

His inductive reasoning seems like really no big deal today,

or do we already know, without a rebirth soon, the whole world will continue to decay?

Finally, Descartes said, "If you thought about it, at least you had a chance."

Did he mean the rest of us would never even give it a fleeting glance?

Socrates said, "Watch out" because he knew that they would all be in our ear.

Aren't we all just a little more confused the moment they all get here?

If Heraclitus's only fragments left pounded the thought that, "No one could step in the same river again" (twice),

then how are we ever supposed to know where to even begin?

With self-consumed totalitarians scared of real philosophical progress all along,

should we just thank Locke, who defined our natural rights linked to a way we could all belong?

With friction all around us, that is why they played down Kant's Duty and Reason,

because they did knew bad things were on the way, so it would be a very short season.

Then they had to push Mill's concept that it "could be good for us all" as the potential last stand,

because they knew a great rationalization was never really a big plan!

We were all upset when we learned Nietzsche tried to divide us by his great big split,

or can we assume maybe he was actually just already spent?

I know many said it was a combination of what they all said at one point in time…

But can we assume that they actually just ran out of time?

Remember Parmenides's only poem told us the only truth was that "All change was actually a total illusion."

Or did Christ actually prove that he was just in some kind of delusion?

Written on February 16th, 2023, on a long talk with my son, Joseph in an intense debate about our quest for what is Absolute Truth mean in the end?

4. Our Lonely Walk!

We all start with unlimited hope and joy,

but we are quickly reminded that we are just a boy.

The mediocre mob slowly kills our special high,

yet we later learn they really don't even know why.

Our dreams were really all about who we thought we wanted to be.

not what we could actually really see.

With cliche 'never give up' reminders swirling all around,

you realize this was never your town.

We chose to rally like Pavlov's dogs,

Or just join the crowded, medicated fogs.

Early Rationalizations along the way

may help you; keep away some of the slow decay.

We all learn to live with anxiety, disillusionment, and fear as rooms in our minds

until we finally make up our ultimate minds.

When passion finally reignites like you are a little boy all over again, you cherish this time like it has always been.

As times starts to speed by faster,
you start realizing you were never really your own master.

Then we realize even in your tethered last stand
that God did have a much better plan.

After your private darkness converts to inner peace, in the end
you can finally see your perfect Zen.

Remember the human spirit must suffer enough along the way,
or we could never see our anointed day!

Written by Joe Steier after talking with some long term Kentucky Business Leaders who had a run of unplanned bad luck in the lobby of KY HOF Ceremony Nov 22

5. Winning and Losing

'Winning and Losing' was the ultimate fork in the road,

but for many of us there is still a private code.

The first time you finally go all the way to see if you can really win,

the isolation may already be setting in.

People drop out after round 1 because they feel the extreme cold.

But never for the ones who remain ferociously bold.

'Winning and Losing' are more random than we first deemed to be true,

maybe divided by a vote, one signature, or a random play by the unaffiliated crew.

The Victors are overly championed when earning their crowning due,

yet the growing bandwagon of followers never even had a clue.

Maybe the closely defeated had equal blood and sweat infused the whole way,

but fate just would not let it be their defining day.

The dueling parties are treated so differently in the end,

yet the work and the passion may have been the same within.

So after both groups are clearly divided by Noah's parted sea,

the quitters drift away with no choice but to just let it be!

The ones who stay down only have one thing to consider; how will it feel to just slowly wither.

The boldly defeated will rally and move forward without rational reason,

always knowing they need to have their own season.

Many say it never really mattered after all, but did they ever really answer their call?

'Winning and Losing' may just be fate for the day,

and yet we celebrate like it is the only way.

Written on plane to Steamboat January 2023 after reflecting on our son, Luke, who fought some challenging odds early on in his life, and yet always gets back up after every set back he experiences to win in the end as an inspiration to our family.

6. Faith

It starts as a mythical fable to you.
It was never real, but it was to you.

It moves around like it owns you.
It slips away but never abandons you.

It can be consuming but way too ethereal for you.
It has no boundaries, so it never stops pinging you.

It is everywhere yet nowhere to you.
It looks like a rainbow that wants to be with you.

It looks so big sometimes that it consumes you.
It is not even there when your reality distorts you.

It was sold as an undeniable right to you.
It was so misunderstood that it overwhelms you.

It is so vast and elusive that it confuses you.
It was quite simple and always ready for you.

Written on plane from Chicago on Feb 1st, 2033.

7. Mandela's Soul

Back then the debate remained oceans away,

which is why it seemed to die the very next day.

'Apartheid' was an overwhelming word for that season,

but if you remember, the debate always had a great reason.

Colonization became sins from our own historical past,

but many of us assumed that it did not even last.

We were all so stunned when we could finally see in;

that is when we all realized we did not know where to even begin.

My girlfriend shut down her school with a sit-in protest to make a point,

but everyone we knew always supported the joint.

My dad was so focused on the union battle at home

that we rarely saw eye-to-eye on the new battle zone.

Great injustices like these need a leader that will die for the new dream,

or Nelson could have never build that kind of team.

Two decades later, we arrived in Cape Town to see "the just new world,"

but the promised land was still covered in the great new swirl.

We were all shocked from the aftermath of his greatest victory,

but soon realized to many, it was still somewhat contradictory.

We all wanted to walk his sacred path and celebrate the "one of a kind,"

but then we realized we were almost out of time.

Intense prayer vigils started while world leaders from around the globe covered his town.

It was then that we could all see his spiritual crown.

Many looked at us as we witnessed his sacred passing.

I just hope no thought we were just trespassing.

To study something from a textbook when I was a totally different being,

then to know finally what I was seeing—

I learned to turn the theorical other cheek, but believed before this day it was just for the meek!

Written after Cape Town, South Africa, family visit to attend a Mandela's prayer vigil and after his passing, December 2013

8. The Great Cardinal Sin

I cannot remember my first priestly greeting,

but I never thought all of us would take such a devastating beating.

We walked to the altar to receive our first communion,

thinking it was a one-of-a-kind spiritual union.

We trembled in the line before each private confessional session,

never knowing the MAN behind the wall may have had a greater transgression.

The Catholic faith was the greatest pride for all of us back then,

but no one knew of the growing cardinal sin.

Having a second wall of spiritual protection seemed too good to be true,

but it was definitely ruined by the corrupt few.

Scary cracks seemed to show as soon as I can remember,

but you rarely heard it from another church member.

I wondered why our parish and clergy had such a revolving door,

but we never knew of the coming war.

They trained all of us to put the Priest above ALL,

but the Catholic leaders already knew they had missed the moral call.

When I went to Rome by myself to see firsthand,

I soon realized there was already a growing Vatican wasteland.

I went to visit Peter's upside-down tomb;

I can remember starting to feel so much overwhelming doom and gloom.

We all know that Jesus put the trust of His Church in a family man,

because what happened since was never His divine plan.

For centuries "married priests" moved money from collections into personal gain,

but that would have never been this kind of unfixable stain.

All of our families donated so much money per the sacred text, that where it all went now makes us all quite perplexed.

So much that has happened takes me back to St. Augustine's City of God,

where he addressed the first great fraud.

Many of us hope they can sell off all the art and land, so they can finally pay the pain and suffering as a moral stand.

Don't get me wrong, because there are great ones every time we take time to look,

so we can never give up on the Great Book.

I pray now more than ever, in hope that where I go next is forever!

Written after a private meeting with a high-ranking priest who was appalled at all that has happened with the Catholic Church, March 2022

9. Remember when…

It started with three fantasy books that we all thought were true:

The Bible, *The Night Before Christmas*, and *Zooey's Zoo*!

Opening my half-shade, looking for it over the morning dew,

but squinting slightly because I did not even have a clue.

A backyard circus of wonder and joy that I have not seen since,

a little painful every time I try to reminisce.

Loved that season the most, even if it ended without a true toast.

All over after a rotary phone call from a room away,

It would take too long to explain what happened on that day.

I had pulsating angst from something that I never slowed down enough to see,

but I knew now it was never going to be.

Many ask how you really know,

if they all protected us from seeing the real show.

I still know for certain what I needed was never really there,

because I never felt that piercing stare.

With Mom finally resting inside, I think it is finally that time.

I took off as fast as I could with prized records and favorite books along for the ride,

but actually knowing I would never made it to the other side.

There were doors I could never open or stairs I would never go down,

even if they could never hear a sound.

There are reasons way too complex to explain away,

so I just waited until it was too late on the very last day.

So many questions I wanted answered but never weighed in—

I think I know now what it might have been.

Drafted in June 10th coming home from Miami after reflecting on two events that drastically eliminated by childhood joy and innocence

10. C.G.'s AMAZING LIFE

I stopped to look back at the church as I watched it finally empty out,

knowing his legacy, both far and wide, was never in doubt!

Memories, stories, and lessons being told by the whole crowd—

but you would never hear him make a braggadocious sound.

From the time I came back, it seemed everyone wanted to be under his tent. Then, if you made it, your best days would be called #lifewithclint.

His personal loyalty, his honor for heritage, and his passion for winning where always part of your cherished time with him; all just hoping these days would never end!

He carried family expectations as a heavy badge of valor the best he could, and like every "other only son" thinks he should.

Horse racing may have been his greatest passion and favorite game, that for all of us going to the track will never be the same.

His lion's heart seemed to always be present on every bet and play, until the games end for that amazing day.

He knew competing was life's process that might let us stay a timeless boy, but it was after the grind that he brought all of us so much joy.

Today you will see initials "CG" on tennis shorts at his alma mater, or being worn on the Bellarmine Knight Jersey's as a badge of honor.

Our famed Churchill Downs will never feel the same for most of us for many seasons, but as you can understand now it is for obvious reasons.

Stories will be shared for years to come, but we all know a life like that can never be truly redone!

Written after attending Clinton Glasscock's funeral in the parking lot across from his packed church service on August 2023

11. Death One by One.

From a premature passing that shocked his world,

he never forgot the pain he endured.

Dad kept the names on a list called his "faithfully departed,"

and that's how I think it all started.

He would pull out his cherished list so often

that I honestly became haunted by my own future coffin.

He would demand that we pray for all of them like our own kin,

until they all somehow got in.

Every meal was the same way, and it just became another day.

It seemed so heavy as a spiritual ritual to learn early on,

but THANK GOD we learned how to be present as each one was gone.

The list grew faster when I look back at how Dad memorialized it all,

but I think he was showing all of us we would be ready for his own call.

All of those years, I remember him on his knees at church every day and night, I would usually watch with only one eye to never be in his sight.

The list had three columns until he started to write them on the back side of the page, making us realize it was the final stage.

As he feared he might be next, my father "faithfully departed" list and their "private prayers" cards filled up his entire sacred text.

He believed every one's passing had to be revered and validated by their own deeds;
Sometimes it was just a slow rosary counting all of the sacred beads.

Somehow, he made us all believe this would come back to us when we needed it most, but I honestly believe he discerned we would all need the votes!

Written in July 2009 after my father's passing where we purchased full page newspaper add to share his faith and journey.

12. The Adoptive Search

They were all around us in the great big secret code.

Maybe, all of us came in one big boatload.

Before Roe vs. Wade,

big Catholic orphanages and adoption agencies ruled the day.

I learned the devastating news from a birth certificate mistake.

When the baseball coach called me out, I started to shake.

I drove home crying on my bicycle, and I could barely see the road,

thinking with every pedal turn that my heart might implode.

I saw Mom in the front yard planting seasonal flowers,

but the awkward conversation seemed like it lasted for hours.

She convinced me so that I might believe I was the only one,

but Mom said, "Be careful with our secret, or you might get shunned."

We all kept this to ourselves until great big sleepovers,

and then it got shared in the dark under our bedcovers.

Zabel, Noe, Curran, Benton, just to name the first few,

then I tried to build an adoptive crew.

I think back now that it seems like it may have been every fifth house, but maybe my paper route was a way to eliminate any doubt.

Many of our "chosen group" fought some addictive battles for as long I can remember, but at least we all felt like charter members.

Some of us stumbled upon the rare, thick manila envelope the parents hoped you would never find, but most of us feel blessed today that we declined.

I saw the name of a fifteen-year-old mother's name as I opened my personal cover, and realized the strength of a little girl who I was so grateful to, the one time I did go undercover.

There was no father's name listed, so I really will never know if he even existed.

The ones who would never let it go, seemed they wish they never went so far to see the painful show.

After hearing tragic and shocking stories over and over again, I realized it was better to never let that "let's try to meet them" process begin.

There are some rooms that we should never enter, because if you do, you will never lose the great tormentor.

Thinking about my amazing parents for the rest of our season, I really did not need to know, for whatever reason.

Once you realize that you were blessed beyond belief, it actually become a great private relief.

I started visualizing Miss America and a neurosurgeon on a great one-night stand, and maybe that was what God had planned!

I am not going to lie, but I think I actually saw him once. I followed him for a pulsating hour, acting like a moving wallflower.

It's really too late now to even look back as the season has come to the end, and I have no more energy left to expend.

Mary Louise and Elmer seem so perfect as I try to parent today, knowing when St Joseph's called 491-9788, it was truly my Lord's Day!

Written after making a donation and reflecting back to St. Joseph's Catholic Charities and Orphanage amazing impact prior to Roe vs Wade decision in July, 2020

13. Ray's Fever from Hell

He always possessed a kind heart that you rarely see.

I remember wishing that it was actually me.

He loved rock-n-roll but never understood a word on the sheet.

I read the lyrics over and over again and could not find a beat.

He had no enemies that really came to mind.

I was only trying to learn to be color blind.

He stayed so close to home that he never really left.

I went far away just to see if I could pass my own acid test.

He always studied hard, just to belong.

I only studied certain things so I would not be wrong.

He seemed so happy at the simplest of things.

I thought we talked about actually being kings.

He was so handsome, but he never believed it for a day.

I was always envious of him in every way.

He never had any complicated thoughts or issues to fight.

I just wish God would give us a do-over on that 'ill-fated night.'

He reached a 104-105 fever pitch in the blink of an eye.

When I left that afternoon, I never said goodbye.

He could not remember anything 67 days later.

I know he would have died without the ventilator.

His seizures were so violent by the time reality set in.

I know all of us felt like NOT rushing to the ER—that night was our real sin.

He lived the rest of his life as one continuous untimed day.

I cried over and over through the years as we watched the slow decay.

He drank his iced tea continuously with burning cigarettes in his off hand.

I think we all knew the doctors had tried various things but had no real plan.

He played the same Zeppelin tunes like the songs were just released.

I remember him re-crying about everyone who was already deceased.

He seemed to stay 23 as his body was ravaged, seizure by seizure.

I was always inspired that he stayed a true believer.

The fever from hell was something that broke my parents' spirit.

I know for sure because I could actually hear it.

I feel like I watched the fever burn down all that my parent's had

left, but maybe it was just a brutal test?

The fever changed our family in so many unfortunate ways.

that as brothers there were no more good days.

Written after my brother's passing during COVID at our Signature Healthcare Facility on August 2020.

FYI - My brother, Ray, had a 104-105 temp for 24 hours that created brain swelling and grandma seizures that put him in a coma during my senior year of college, where he never recovered. He slowly lost all of his childhood friends, fiancé, and his ability to live independently, all from this 36-hour high fever episode that ruined a great life with amazing potential. He was beyond special and had the kindest heart that drew people in. His illness was something our family never recovered from.

14. World Peace?

We prayed for it daily as our allegiance pledge, not really knowing what we really said.

In the very beginning, it seemed far-far away, but it did not matter as a small boy having the perfect day.

We learned to worship men of our armed service from the very beginning, because who else was undefeated in every inning?

We spent more time playing Cowboys and Indians, which would have me cancelled today, and to even think I was given a game board once based upon the "blue vs the grey."

Maybe little boys thought the biggest problems were from our own troubled past, but we had never even seen our first newscast.

There was a time when "civil disobedience" started to make some amazing progress that was rare for the season, but many believed it was a weak concept for obvious reasons.

I had pulsating childhood nightmares I remember from the Cold War, but it was Reagan and Gorbachev that we all came to adore.

When the famed wall finally went down, I believed the Pope, Russia, and the US would always be on solid ground.

It now seemed possible for an extended point in time, until we get pulled into the next few dictators' heinous crimes.

The dreamy state was lost when three genocides (Bosnia, 92-95; Rwanda, 94; Congo, 96-97) were all front and center, and it was now something we all had to consider.

In the end, with two million murdered, you had to assume it would be another unifying worldwide charter.

Our 9/11 was the day that haunts us all, but we were hoping it would be our last big military call.

I remember Bush celebrating the initial Uprising transitioning to an Arab Spring, as we all thought about what it might bring.

As democracy was pushed out farther and wider than any one government had ever considered, it actually backfired in ways that we should all remember.

That Spring passed quickly in all the places that it really mattered (in Yemen, Libya, Iraq and Syria), and our biggest dream was now shattered.

Evil leaders, oppressed people, and unstable governments now cover nearly half of the global land—how can we not feel like we are all in our own quicksand?

No words of history that I read on my high school page could really humanize the pain we witness today.

With twenty years of failures and 2.9 trillion spent on both the Afghan War and the Arab Spring, can we finally re-learn some lessons over again?

Is it time to turn inward and force our leaders to get along again, or is that now too toxic to happen again?

Ukraine, Israel, Syria, Iraq, China and North Korea just to name a troubling few—is there any chance now for a peaceful coup?

Written in September of 2021 after the US Troop withdrawal from Afghanistan on August 30,2021

15. The Great Commonwealth

The Great Commonwealth, Long ago

Long ago, there was only one road to choose.
I looked for a very different path,
but you had to be willing to lose.

Long ago, there was only one way
down the glimmering proverbial hall.
When you tried to walk away,
many hoped you would fall.

Long ago, my bricklayer father left me
with haunting words for sure,
but I could just never find the exact cure!

Long ago, the starting point was that
your world would definitely be thinned,
but at that time, it was almost considered a cardinal sin.

Long ago, there were no real books or formulas to even follow,
and once you stepped out,
you better figure out quickly or
you would surely be swallowed.

Long ago, I searched high and low for the keys
to the secret spirited club, and
then realized we were all being snubbed.

Long ago, there were pioneering owners
who controlled the great big ball,
but how could you respect them
and still answer your call?

Long ago, when lifetime jobs started to disappear,
they came calling out for all of us
to reappear.

Today the world may look like
Atlas is really shrugging
like Ayn Rand once predicted,
but it will be all of us who make them stand corrected.

Today we are all here to celebrate
the new options for everyone's personal walk,
but we know for sure it is no longer just talk.

Today because many great pioneers have paved the way for "the all," it is not nearly as hard to answer your call.

Today I can touch the special spirit almost everywhere I go.

It gives me great joy to see all the new ways everyone can now grow.

Today we see the changing commonwealth as a place to soar,

and the great ones I study never keep score.

Today, negative pulsating issues may carry the media's day,

but it is our entrepreneur's unbridled spirit that will pave the new way!

Thanks to everyone for the amazing award, and God Bless all of you and the Commonwealth!

Written for Hall of Fame induction speech in Louisville on November 15th, 2017

16. Our Town

It may start on a Little League Baseball Diamond in a middle-class Hikes Point neighborhood, with two eleven-year-old pitchers—one for the Dodgers, the other for the Cubs—and becomes a sacred phone call three decades later, which triggers the founding of a revolutionary company.

It may start during a first business transaction between two neighborhood boys with sweaty hands in the corner of a cold garage trading a 56 Ted Williams for a Mickey Mantle rookie…that becomes a chance reconnection thirty-two years later and a fresh look at one's hometown.

It may start between high school classmates who spiritually bond, serving in their first wedding party together for the former King and Queen of the prom…which links a destined introduction to a visionary university president, unleashing a new way to think about healthcare innovation.

It may start with three childhood friends who have finally earned their "first real job" and now seek to help the homeless, who meet a dynamic young woman to lead the cause…who all reunite two decades later for an idea festival that ignites everyone to think beyond the scope of possibility.

It may start with two seven-year-old boys dreading their summer swim lessons… which later crests with a group of similar thinking thought leaders who found Louisville's new blue ocean of endless jobs.

It may start with struggling non-conformist high school adolescents dreaming of personal freedom but who constantly receive "Edisonian rejection,"…which translates into a company headquarters' city-wide celebration 26 years later because they had the trust of their partners to see the new vision for the city.

It may start with four high school paper boys who worked 365 days a year, validated by their first presidential letter from a man named Ronald, who was already dreaming of being the next David.

It may take one really sick child for a father to understand the spiritual wealth of a community and the power of prayer to write a book and launch God in the workplace six years ago…that after a 12000-mile journey to the promised land, he might hope to be a spiritual addition to the international festival of faiths.

It may take one Catholic college on a hill which, after decades of steady leadership, encouraged by the brightest minds to stay at "home" and learn the art of "soulful business,"…which inspires leaders to dream of a new "Mertonian" leadership center, transforming the corporate mindset into an international beacon of light for the world to see.

It may start with cities that could not hear a company's sleepless hopes to fulfill the dreams of its people for a GED to Ph.D. program of intellectual prosperity…while a hometown had already matched the dream to its visionary path.

It might finally start to come together with key stakeholders from both coasts during cold winter days and nights and several committed California families saying "yes"—this was the fertile ground for revolution.

Perhaps it starts from an array of life's relationships combined with an intimate crossroads of Godly purpose, uniting drive and desire into the harvest of opportunity.

…And it finally happens that hundreds of great leaders standing together in faith and hope in that same town that decades later becomes the City of Possibilities and the Idea Capital of the world.

Written by Joe Steier on the Grand opening of SHC Headquarters on October 11, 2010

17. Sweet Sixteen

Dads watch their lives go speeding by, always asking GOD *why?*

Dads must survive the daily grinding,

hoping that them and their baby girls' hearts are slowly binding.

Dads try to relive their lives through their boys,

but they spoil their little girls with all the right toys.

Dads always hope that their little girl will keep them as the "apple of their eye."

Knowing you, try to build them so one day they can fly.

Dads cherish their little girls like nothing else ever,

and they know it is truly their most noble endeavor.

Dads will always guard their little girl like precious gold,

while quietly building them to be beautiful and bold

Dad carries many burdens that are somewhat unknown,

but only a little girl makes them feel like a king where they can sit on their temporary throne.

Dads never really like the concept of another boy someday taking over, but they support, secretly hoping one day they might get another four-leaf clover (granddaughter).

Dads know little girls are truly spiritual gems that change your life from day one, dreading the day the little girl phase is actually done!

Dads sit around talking incessantly about their girls 24/7,

hoping that their good work was enough to get them into Heaven!

Happy Sweet 16, Poem to my daughter Jacqueline Christine Rose Steier, May 2008

18. Belize.....

In my garage one summer day, working on my birthday giveaway...

I sometimes had a conflicted ping that became a quiet, constant ting.

I had some inspiring sources showing how to serve all, but when you are a kid, you can't really hear the call.

Finally, a private prayer said something in me that planted GOD's first mustard seed....

Now it was so obvious that I could truly see people in need....

With my feeling a little teenage doubt, GOD gave me a great shout out: "GO to Belize and Build Me a House."

After a ten-page instruction guide, five days of sweaty work, and an endless list of "to-do's,"

we celebrated like a whole new family with brand new views.

Finally at the end of it all, God said, "Rest, my team, because you answered my call."

How could such a small beam fulfill such a big dream?

In the end, I will never be the same because of all the lessons I gained!

Written by Jacqueline Steier (age 7) with her Dad, Joe Steier on her birthday weekend.

19. Caroline's Canaries

On her back porch that was the envy of too many,

it seemed like she was raising her own little city.

Like any great show act, Caroline's Canaries—as they were named—

never really knew of their fame.

The connected flock sung like an orchestra all day.

Everyone was wishing they would come their way.

Little precious yellow feathers that looked as soft as a dove,

something Grandma Limbach surely loved.

Her backyard sounded like a 50-piece band

that only a few neighbors could not stand.

Every time Grandma Limbach got a little down,

all she had to do was hear her sound.

Watching the Canaries dancing in the air

made every little child stare.

Sadly, they were not for Grandma Linebach to keep,

because she always knew the price was too steep.

Written by Jacqueline Steier (Age 10) with her Dad to honor Father Linebach, her childhood priest mother, who passed away .... April 2011

20. Mom's Final Request; Forgiveness is Freedom

We learn from Peter's *seven times seven,*

As maybe our best path to Heaven.

I often thought, *What the hell happened to him?*

And then years later, I did not even know where to begin.

'Christ-like' was too far away from someone as confused as me;

it was validated by my father, who never left his own knees.

So many disingenuous confessions that they say were a must,

That I really never knew who to trust.

When I went further off track, things definitely became worse.

It was so bad for a while that I thought I might be cursed.

The brutal 'close to home' hits were all stabs to the hardening heart.

At one point, I just wanted to find a way for a 'child-like' fresh start.

My mom's deathbed advice was, "Son, please let it ALL go, as a final favor to me."

Haunting words from 'True Saint' that someday might be.

She had some painful things happen to her, and yet never wanted her redemption or her due,

Because she was as Christ-like as anyone I ever knew.

I learned about most of the unjust things from what was never really said.

They left some letters and a private note for me that I never actually read.

On a pulsating final drive home, I knew she could see inside my soul.

Devious Gary, Imposter Mitch, Lying Julie, Dirty Brian, and Pathological Steve had ALL taken their toll.

In retrospect, she taught me it was about setting me free,

than using ALL of that pent up hatred to hyper-motivate me.

Then I remembered a doctor from years back who f- - - - up our new born son, and family but acted like a saint,

But when your son is fighting for his life, you have to show some restraint.

Before Luke's miraculous healing, that doctor still remained an absolute no,

But after an issue-clearing phone call with him, I decided I had to finally let that go.

If you ever try to make this mythical and scary climb,

You will feel naked, free, and restored ALL in one moment in time.

Many said, "The Holy Spirit sounds beyond interesting, but where is the old you?"

But I doubt they really loved me, or ever had the slightest clue.

Privately, I cried so hard the week of her sacred passing,

Because what she requested I knew I had to make happen!

But if we look closely, Christ was always preparing us this ultimate test—

I actually thank them ALL now, because I can finally have some peace and rest!

First Drafted in the fall of 2011 after a long talk with my mother, Mary Louise Steier, after her terminal illness diagnosis.

21. Happiness is…

www.ingramcontent.com/pod-product-compliance
Lightning Source LLC
LaVergne TN
LVHW010122170826
845678LV00012B/2540

* 9 7 8 1 9 1 7 3 6 7 0 8 0 *